WOUNDED HEARTS

Take a Chance

WOUNDED HEARTS

HEARTS

Take a Chance

ENDLESS SKY

BOOKS

DEBBIE QUIGLEY

WOUNDED HEARTS TAKE A CHANCE

By Debbie Quigley

Endless Sky Books

Regina, Saskatchewan, Canada

www.endless-sky-books.com

Copyright © 2023 by Debbie Quigley

Trade Paperback ISBN: 978-1-989398-72-2

Ebook ISBN: 978-1-989398-73-9

Cover and interior design by Edward Willett

Contents

To all those whose wounded hearts have opened,
and to the men who opened them.

Foreword

This little book is dedicated to all those whose wounded hearts have been shattered into pieces, those who are afraid to take a chance on loving another man. Trust is something that, once broken, is difficult to get back.

If you have had your heart broken into many pieces, you shy away from going through that pain once again. Accepting the fact of aloneness, you don't want to open your heart to loving another man

Aloneness is a way of protecting your heart, of building up walls to ensure hurt never again penetrates your heart. Having built up walls of safety when infidelity and betrayal are involved, it's much harder to trust again.

Taking a chance to fall in love again, to trust again, to let another into your life and possibly feel love and passion once again, is a big leap. Let me take you along the poetic, romantic path of a woman opening her heart to loving again.

It all started one fine summer's day when a first-glance attraction walked into her yard . . .

Being Alone

A simple, protected life
Keeping walls around her heart
Listening to the sound of her own voice
Drying her own tears.

Simple and peaceful, it seems to be
Being alone
Not the way it should be
Life is worth living!

Listening to another's voice
Having her tears dried by someone else
At the end of a sad movie or when sad news arrives
Peaceful is a good way to live.

Simple is a way of life
Not as much fun when all alone!
Magic is a campfire

DEBBIE QUIGLEY

Gazing at the stars at night
Sharing this beauty
Holding a warm hand
We all want that as much as we deny it.

Being alone for her was easy, she thought
Protecting her shattered heart from another scar
Living alone was simple and peaceful
Better when shared with another.

Hugs and kisses during the day and after dark
Letting another man into your life
Taking a chance to love again!

Men and women need each other
Being alone is not all it is cracked up to be!
Let someone in your life!
It might just be worth the risk!
Loving is living!

Being alone is not the way it was meant to be!
The man you take a chance on just might be the one
Putting sunshine into your alone life.

Loving Again When the Marriage Is Over

The day came
Removing the much-loved wedding band
No longer a wife
The marriage was over
Her heart closed to feeling love again.

Time passed
Acceptance, aloneness were part of life
Remembering the days of hugs, kisses, and sharing.

She wondered if she would love again
Feel the passion that would make her feel alive
Life kept her busy, so love was a last thought.

That all changed on a summer's day
She met a man that made her heart throb once again

His eyes looked into her eyes
Sparks of attraction started that day
A single woman once again
She felt something in her clouded soul
A spark had been lit again
Life is not meant to be spent alone.

First-Glance Attraction

Her heart had been closed like a spring bud
Dark clouds preventing the opening of her flowering heart
The dark clouds had separated now, just like a morning fog
She glanced at him—their eyes met
He smiled at her—she smiled back.

A small-statured man with a friendly, inviting smile
He walked slowly toward her and spoke in a gentle tone
Her heart healed from the emotional scars
Now when she looks in the mirror, a strong, confident woman
    stares back
Her eyes now dry from a tear-stained past
She was ready for her flowering heart to open again
To her first-glance attraction.

They chatted
He asked for her phone number
Her heart whispered, *Until we meet again*.

First-Glance Date

This handsome man called
She invited him for dinner
A knock came on her door
Her hands hot from her fast heartbeat
Walking toward the door, opening it
Her first-glance-attraction man stood with a beautiful warm
   smile
His chest hidden by a huge bouquet of wildflowers for her.

She reached for the bouquet; it touched her heart
It had been so long since the beauty of a bouquet was given to her
He wore a black-and-grey striped shirt
Dark pants on his slender body
His smile mesmerized her
Her heart fluttered.

A meal was shared with easy conversation and much laughter

Upon leaving, he pulled her slender body toward his
Hugging her tightly
His hug felt so warm against her.

He reached and stroked her hair and face ever-so-gently
Those feelings had been locked away for so long
A great first date!

The door to her heart had opened
The attraction for each other was mutual
Passion felt in the hug
Feelings that had been trapped in her heart
Now unleashed!

Her heart looks forward to the next date
With the man with a first-glance attraction.

Man of Desire

A light now shone in her heart
His tender touches opened a closed door
Her heart beats from processing their time together
A friendship of first-glance attraction
Her heart melts when he smiles at her
She dreams of real love in her life
Exhilarated excitement enters her focus
Words of trust being built
Each word a brick of trust
Bringing her to the point of slowly tearing down the walls
    around her heart.

She wants to trust and love again, taking each step toward it
Cautious in her steps
Loving each minute they spend together.

Butterflies that had lived dormant in her so long
Now flutter as her heart expands from his tender touch

His tender touch engulfs her in thoughts of desire and passion.

The night of passion comes
She sheds her outer coverings to allow the rapture of lovemaking
A night of intimacy they shared
She feels comfortable and safe with this man
Feelings of tenderness. Her heart is full of light
Love is beginning to enter her soul.

The weeks and months pass, loving each moment spent With
this man of desire who allowed her to see into his heart He,
in return, has touched hers
Two hearts now mingle.

Clouds of Passion

One look!
One gentle touch!
Feelings of intimacy shared
Memories of love clouded her mind
Her heart pounded.
Feelings of his tight body close to hers
Passion running through her veins
Flowing through each part of her body
Heart-pounding loving moments
Tender kisses and caring, sharing, laughter
Run through each vein to the door that opened in her heart.

She shielded her heart, body, and soul for a long time
Not allowing any intimacy with a man
Being alone was something she had accepted as part of her life
Fearful to let someone into her wounded soul.

Falling In Love

It is that special something you feel when looking at another
That person who brings out the best in you
Makes you feel that you are most precious
A friendship that is built with time and trust
The shared moments of laughter
Sensations that are felt when touched by the other
Looking at that face that you do not tire of
A feeling that is the right thing for you.

There are many types of love
Love of family, children, and friends
The deepest love is the love between a man and a woman
One that surpasses all other loves while on this journey of life
Five minutes, five hours, or five seconds are important
    moments during the day or evening
Holding hands, walking down a path in the woods
The beauty of nature, sun shining through the leaves

DEBBIE QUIGLEY

Angel rays shining through the tall trees in the darkness of the
   woods.

This man holds your hand. It is magic!
It warms the heart and soul in that moment of time
A feeling of falling in love
One that you hope continues
Missing him when he is not around
Waiting to hear his voice and see his warm smile
A voice you do not tire of
The safe feeling you have when together
His touch so gentle
We all want this love in our lives.

If you have such a person in your life, hang onto them every
   second and minute
Love is twinkling eyes, warm touches that engage all senses
The feel of his skin against yours
The man holds you tight; he loves your heart and all it holds
Loves you for just you!

New Moments Making Memories

Each moment in life creates a memory
Love each moment of each day
Each moment lived, each second
Moments later becomes a memory
Sharing moments, making memories
Leave the past in the past
Create a new moment of love in life
Moments of sharing, caring, loving
Pack away the luggage of the past
Start a new collection of magic moments
Loving again!

Trust in a new love; give it a chance
Loving again can be a wonderful moment of creation!
Write a new chapter in your book of life
Turn the page and make new chapters

DEBBIE QUIGLEY

Moments of savouring that love feeling
Embrace it with your heart.

Make moments that are everlasting!
It is a come-alive moment
One shared between two.

Write the next chapters in your life
Include new memories with your new man

Walk In the Woods

Walking along a manmade path
Trees the size of skyscrapers touch the sky
Dots of blue overhead peek through.

Walking through the forest
Together with his love, his four-legged friends
Join in harmony, marching on
Warm rays from the sun pierce the branches, light filtering
    down
On pinecones and their needles, leaves all around.

The silence and stillness were what was shared
Dogs running ahead, not looking back
Tails waving like flags in the air.

Twigs snapped as each footstep was taken
Trees that had fallen covered nature's floor
The forest floor held its own design

Dead stumps with holes, a home for little animals that were
    not seen
Rocks of all sizes, here and there
Rock cuts, high and deep, were included in the deep woods
Pictures of pleasure for eyes to see
Rocks covered with blankets of green moss, each a unique
    design
Mushrooms of all hues added colour bright
To nature's browns on the deep-woods floor.

Dogs that he loved became friends
They shared him in their comfort zone as she joined in.

Nature's forest, untouched and natural
Similar feelings in her heart, natural and beautiful
The fresh smells of the forest air, fresh and clean
Walking along, entering the maze of trees that had fallen
Tree soldiers dead on the ground
A maze of unknown territory
Sharing sheer simplicity and comfort
On a walk with him and his four-legged friends
In nature's beauty, untouched and real.

Once again, back at the starting point, his home in the woods
A home that is shared with his four-legged friends
They all shared the day and the forest walk
It was beautiful and simple
A man of the woods shared his loves that day.

Reoccurring Dream

His smile is a reoccurring dream
That plays repeatedly
Taking her to a place of joyful bliss
She dreams of that boyish smile that she loves to see
It ends with her arms wrapped around him so tight

The reoccurring dream of that smile warms her heart
It's a dream she cannot wait to see
A dream without end, she hopes it to be.

His smile is endless with comfort
It fills her heart with love
That beautiful smile
In her reoccurring dream

Her Open Heart She Shares with Him

You just stay being you
Open and honest
Keeping it real and simple
Open hearts sharing
Nothing false, no masks.

I am just me
You keep being you
Flaws accepted.

We are not perfect
Perfection is a myth
Let us just be
Who we are today
Loving the open honesty we share.

I love the fact you love my open heart
Willing to view the scars it holds
I am just me.

Your heart lets me peer in
I love the man I see
The kindness and gentle spirit in your heart and soul
Just keep being you
The man that holds my heart today
A man that shares my laughter.

You hold me with your gentle touch
Express your heart and just love me for being me
You truly are the one for me!

Coupled Friendship

Sometimes, you meet a special person on life's journey
You just seem to click
Their smile makes you smile
They feel the same way about subjects
They seem to know what you are thinking
Without you saying a word.

You share comfort when you are together
Relaxed and free from the world's stresses
You can just be you!

Comfy sweaters, jeans, and big boots
Nothing attractive about that, you think
It does not matter to him.

Coupled friendship of love and trust
Grateful for meeting this man
He adds to your happiness in everyday life

Your lover, friend, and companion.

The coupled friendship that you
Never experienced previously in life
Coupled friendship; true love!

Hand to Hold

When we were little girls, we all held our father's hand
A hand of safety, we felt.

Years pass by. Many hands we hold
Sometimes never feeling that safety again.

Many of us wait a lifetime for that special hand
That we all hope to hold again
One that gives a feeling of safety and love
The hand of strength, friendship, and love
A hand that holds special meaning when placed over his heart.

That hand holds memories of each time together that you have
   shared
My hope is that you find that special
Hand to hold!

Wounded Hearts Take a Chance

I hope you enjoyed this little book, a poetic journey into
  loving again
A romantic twist to engulf your heart and awaken your soul
Including the beauty of nature's peaceful simplicity, shared
  with another.
My goal with my whisper-art is to chart a poetic path
To the possibility of loving again.

Wounded hearts, now that your hearts have been warmed
Open your heart to the possibility of loving again.

I, too, was a wounded heart with scars from a broken past
I decided to take a leap of faith. You can, too!
Maybe, just maybe, you will meet a man that opens your heart
  today!

Warm fuzzies,
Debbie

About the Author

Debbie Quigley, born in Peterborough, Ontario, Canada, is the author of *Wind Whispers*, a collection of poetry available on Amazon. Debbie loves to touch hearts with her whisper-art poetry. A retired healthcare worker, Debbie lives in a small hamlet surrounded by nature and wildlife. She loves to garden.

Her poetry is simple and real, telling a story in her poetic whisper-art form. Debbie has contributed to Spiritual Writers Network publications. Her poetry can also be found on Author's Den. If you wish to comment on this publication, email Debra at debbiequigley2001@hotmail.com.

BOOKS

Founded by award-winning author Edward Willett, Endless Sky Books is an eclectic hybrid publisher of all kinds of books, from children's books to poetry to fiction to nonfiction.

Find out more about Endless Sky Books on our website, endless-sky-books.com, and visit our traditional sister publisher, Shadowpaw Press, at shadowpawpress.com.